A DIFF

Walter
Bauer

ENT SUN

Translated from
the German by
Henry Beissel

An Oberon Book

ISBN 0 88750 165 6

Printed in Canada

PUBLISHED IN CANADA BY OBERON PRESS

WALTER BAUER arrived in Toronto from his native Germany in 1952, carrying in his luggage half a century of Europe that included two world wars and the Nazi holocaust that linked them. Packed neatly alongside these public disasters were his personal experiences that began as a labourer's fifth child in Merseburg in Saxony in 1904, continued with the bitter struggle to survive the hungry years of the twenties and reached a first peak of success with the appearance of four books, two volumes of poetry and two novels, in the years just preceding the Nazi takeover. The critics hailed him as a bright new star in the literary sky. But with Hitler a black night fell upon Germany in which all stars were extinguished. As a left-wing writer Bauer was lucky to escape with his life. His books were banned, and for twelve years he watched with hatred and despair as barbarism dragged Europe into the very pit of hell. He staggered from the ruins of the Third Reich covered with the shame of his people but driven by a desperate determination to help build a new world—"a human world for man to live in." In the space of seven years after his return from a prisoner-of-war camp, he published 26 books, including plays, poetry, biographies, essays and a novel, all of them in one way or another calling for a return to sanity, to civilization, to the fellowship of men. In 1956, Bauer reached a second peak of fame when he was awarded the Albert Schweitzer Prize for Literature for his biography of Nansen.

Ironically, his passionate plea for "a human world" had broken national barriers precisely at a time when he himself had ceased to believe in the possibility of a free and socially just Europe. His disillusionment came as international communism revealed its brutality on the one hand, while on the other the German bourgeoisie quickly returned to its habits of ruthless greed. Walter Bauer decided to put an ocean between himself and his "desperate love" of Europe, whose agonies he couldn't bear to watch any longer. For the third time in his life he started from scratch to carve out a new existence for himself, this time of his own accord.

Today Bauer is Canada's immigrant poet *par excellence*, and the fact that he is still relatively little known in this country is part of the evidence to prove it. His 24 years in Toronto are true to the immigrant archetype: the steady climb up the social ladder starting at the bottom—in his case, from dishwasher to university professor. More to the point, the twenty books he has published since his arrival in Canada have all been written in German. Here lies one of the main sources of the immigrant's alienation: the virtual impossibility of growing in a second language, as an adult, that intricate network of roots that reaches far below the conscious mind. The consequences for a writer are grave, limiting his access to new experience, obstructing the transformation of that experience in terms of the perceptual systems and hidden myths of the community to which they belong, and perhaps most important of all, isolating him from his true potential readers —the people about whom he writes.

Nine of Bauer's recent books are specifically Canadian in content: three volumes of poetry and three of short stories (one of them significantly called *Fremd in Toronto—Stranger in Toronto*), biographies of Grey Owl and the Sieur de la Salle, and a Canadian diary. None of them has appeared in translation—except for a selection of poems I prepared for Prism International Press in 1968, entitled *The Price of Morning*. As a Canadian writer Bauer still has few readers in Canada because he writes in a foreign language; as a German writer he has fewer and fewer readers in Germany because his preoccupations (which, in the end, are of course also a matter of language) are alien. And there you have the immigrant writer's dilemma in a nutshell.

One recognizes that this double exile is an authentic part of the Canadian experience, and because Bauer's work embodies it so articulately his is (or should be) a major voice in Canadian letters. Most of the poems in this collection were written in Toronto. They are all informed by the tension between the Old World and the New. It is not only the sun that is different here, but the wind and the rain and the train-calls; even "night spreads its wings differently here." This difference is fundamental. It is the difference between despair and hope, between repression and freedom, between past and future—a past that betrayed man, degraded and dehumanized him, and a future in which the best is still possible.

The contrast between *here* and *there* has a deadly edge in these poems, for as a "German of his time" Bauer associates the past with the horrors of the Nazi tyranny. He returns to the subject with terrifying obsessiveness, because to have survived Hitler is to have become, however reluctantly, an accomplice. This stern, puritanical self-judgment is one aspect of his compassion for his fellow men, and it demands the existence of a potentially better world which is, as it must be, projected into the future and identified, for Bauer, with Canada. That identification is Article One of every immigrant's credo.

The agony of his German past has given Bauer a deep insight into the vulnerability of the human condition. But such insight is always bought at the price of distorting reality. It is simply not true that the Canadian sun "never knew shame." Just ask any Indian! The image is valid in terms of the contrapuntal movement of the poem in which it appears, but the Canada it conjures up is a print made from a Nazi negative, and must therefore contain its flaws in reverse. The poet knows this. One can hear the tremor in his voice as he wonders at the smugness and ignorance of Canadians and considers the possibility that the chance Canada offers the future may be missed or muffed. Nor do these poems propose any blueprint for the future, in spite of the poet's "certainty" about it. Indeed, considering his assurances that "there's still lots waiting to be done around here," this lack of direction is both conspicuous and surprising. It derives both from Bauer's disenchantment with earlier socialist models and from a more general lack of trust in the perfectibility of man. In "Canada" the movement into the future ends in an image of splendid vacuity:

Northern lights
Moving gigantically in flaming silence
Converse about nothing.

These doubts and misgivings modify and correct our perspectives of Canada as a land of natural grandeur and infinite possibilities, and go a long way toward restoring the proportions of the known world. But so long as Bauer submits to the demons of his past, he can never altogether escape the Pilgrim-Fathers syndrome.

On the other hand, to define Walter Bauer as an immigrant poet is to look at a landscape through a keyhole. After all, he was a mature and successful poet long before it occurred to him to settle in Canada, and some of the poems from that period are included in this collection. Their concern with human suffering everywhere shows the poet in revolt against grandiloquent gestures and "big words." His "*Paroles essentielles*" are "bread, milk, meat." No political or philosophical rhetoric will ease the burdens of the living, but only attention to their basic, everyday needs, only loving care for the concrete, mundane anxieties of everyone's existence. As he protests against the rapid dehumanization of our world, the poet speaks with a universal voice that moves and challenges us because we hear in it the pleas of one who knows hunger, deprivation and terror at first hand.

Walter Bauer is not only a poet of our country but also a poet of our time. His experience as an immigrant itself extends his reach beyond our borders, for the heart torn between the country of its childhood and the land that gives it asylum is in tune with an age of dislocation and mass migration in all parts of the globe. Perhaps his anguish is that of the visionary, because, if technological civilization survives, rootlessness will be a condition that man must learn to endure.

In the meantime, these poems demand from us feeling, thought and action. There is no room in them for resignation or despair. Bauer himself, at the age of 72, is far from retiring to a rocking-chair. He has embarked on a new and bold adventure—an arduous journey into a second language. After publishing well over 60 books in German, he is writing his first book in English. "*S'en aller! S'en aller!*" If he insists on reminding us of the past it is only because he knows that a people without a past, without memory, without history, are locked into a vicious circle, and he hopes, undaunted by the massive evidence to the contrary, that men may eventually learn the lessons of their history. His poems are, therefore, what all art ultimately is —an affirmation of the world, a celebration of our foolish, glorious, ridiculous, confused, short, precious, lonely, cheap and magnificent lives.

HENRY BEISSEL

I

The Sun Here

The sun here must be a different sun
From the one under which I used to live.
The sun here has seen forests and rivers,
The long crawl of primeval ages,
And then the slow invasion of the stillness by voices—
Not the end of cities burning to ashes like useless toys,
Not the flames in which history becomes tinder,
Not the imprisonment of whole nations,
Not the long treks of undesirables staggering into limbo,
Not the camps like stains no acid can ever remove.
The sun here has seen nothing, nothing at all.

The sun here must be a different sun
From the one under which I could live no longer.
The sun here has heard the cry of eagles
And the patient whispering of ice ages,
The sound of axes, the triumphant whistle of trains—
Not the thunder of Last Judgments returning night after night,
Not the moaning of nations forced to their knees,
Not the sound of shots, or of sighs,
Not the cry for freedom,
The sun here has heard nothing, nothing at all.
The sun here never turned black, never went into hiding, never knew shame.

Strange sun
Under which I walk like someone waking from an illness that lasted too long,
Like someone who has dreamt black dreams for too long and feels
He can rid himself of them.
He wants to be rid of them, wants to be like those
Who've always lived under this sun.
But the dreams come back, every night, after the sun has gone down,
A sun without depth, without shame, without guilt, without shadows.

This Big City

This big city
Where the winds blow from the north
Coldly, indifferently, cutting through thin shirts
(Buy yourself a warmer one, brother)
As though they were yesterday's newspaper—
This big city
Where thousands hunger for their fortune
(*Fortuna* sounds as slippery as fortune and good-luck—
Try to catch it, brother!)—
This big city
Where recently ten men jointly
Made three million dollars
(Don't get upset, wouldn't you do the same,
My Christian brother?)—
This big city
Where the winds blow from the north
(It'll soon be spring, brother)
Is built on firm foundations,
They say.

Smoke Burns in My Eyes

All at once smoke burns in my eyes and makes them tear.
What sort of smoke is it? And here
So far away from the place where it rises. . . .
After all, there are a few thousand miles of straight water
Between here and there, or "the old country," as one gets into the habit of
saying.
But what's here and what's over there when the smoke makes my eyes tear?

It's not the spicy smell of the autumn campfire around which we gathered
In our childhood long ago, tired out from riding dream horses
Across dream prairies—all that was dreaming,
And the potatoes we roasted in the ashes tasted of the wilds.
But when dusk fell we trampled the fire out,
Our Indian feathers came off
And we went home to bright windows as though to the stars.
How could this exquisite smoke ever burn in my eyes?

It's not the campfires of my youth from which this smoke rises,
Those flames by which we rested after a long day's walking,
Having taken on the hills, the rivers, the country roads and the sky—
Such a load makes us pleasantly tired at the end of a day.
It was good to be by the fire after that and watch the sparks fly
Like fleeting stars up to the durable stars,
And one of us—he later died in the war—read aloud from the *Odyssey*.
This good smoke too never burns in the eyes.

Is it the cities that fell to ruins in a hail of bombs
And offered those who flew above them the spectacle of a pyre
On which history was burning while giant heat-storms
Desiccated the living till they were unrecognizable, boiled them, threw them
into the flames,
Those cities where in the end funerals were entirely without tears and
without resurrection—
Does the smoke that makes my eyes tear come from there?

There was a time when that smoke burnt in my eyes, it burns there no longer.
The cities have risen again, though they stand on perilous ground.

So what kind of smoke is this, where does it come from, why is it
So dense that I can't see some of the places any more of which I was fond,
So dark that I can't remove it any more from faces that meant much to me?
Who lay by its fire? Were those who gathered around it resting?
If you can call it rest. . . in those ovens heated with flesh!
But I suppose that's only for people my age, who know
And knew—and this *knew* makes the smoke denser still.
For people my age, yes. . . but not for everybody.

Tomorrow I shall travel west across the North American continent:
Will the smoke follow me?
I shall see the vast plains and the mountains' silver flames:
Will the smoke melt away there and vanish?
And when I dive with a shout of joy into the Pacific ocean
Will my eyes still be tearing?
Yes, it's the kind of smoke that will follow me everywhere.
It'll always be burning in my eyes.

Solitude of Ships

At night, because I couldn't sleep,
I stood on deck
And the wind blew right through me,
Posing many questions and answering none.
Moving continually
The mast touched the stars
And fell back again, in order to return
With its silent green light
Moving continually.
Music drifted across the deck
From the saloon where there was dancing.
From the bar where there was drinking
Voices came in many different languages.
In the shadow of the superstructure
Two lovers embraced
During the whole voyage.
But at night,
Like everything else on earth,
Ships too are solitary.

My Luggage

At every border I was asked
How much money I was carrying.
And of course they were able to check my luggage
To make sure that
Apart from suits, clothing, shoes
And a few other necessary personal items
I carried nothing on which duty had to be paid.
But I took along more
Than they could see
At the borders of blind Europe
(I wasn't even asked for it).
Now that I've arrived
And walk on alien soil and live in Canada
I'll make a laughing-stock of the customs officers
And tell you what I took along,
What I found most burdensome to carry:
My desperate love for Europe.

Arrival in Halifax

I'm no longer young enough
To throw myself on the ground and stammer:
Hail, new land of Canaan!
At the age of 48
You don't come as a scout any more,
Especially not
With such a heritage
Of guilt,
Which I take along everywhere.
My eyes observe coolly now,
Without excessive expectations,
The heart throbs inside.
There's only one thing I ask of you,
Earth of Canada, whose morning greatness I sense:
Don't be too hard on this stranger,
Give him among friendly people
An open sky to breathe.

Canadian Verses

1
During the long night
Of the journey from Halifax to Toronto
The engine of the train
Occasionally uttered a many-voiced cry.
Trains in Canada have a different call,
And night spreads its wings differently here
Right up to the Arctic.
I listened to the cry.
The earth became more lonely
And I saw in the window filled with darkness
My face
Like that of a stranger quickly passing by.

2
Every morning
On my way to work
I pass a small park
Where the morning light
Silently takes a rest from its own raptures.
Every evening
After ten hours' work
I pass there again.
Now night is stretched out asleep
In the park, guarded by lights,
And I don't recognize it anymore.

3
This morning in Sterling Road,
Between factories,
I found a bird feather
And picked it up.
Many had passed there before me. . . .
And it seemed to me
As though the flight-wind still trembled
In the feather, and the drop of water on it
Was the condensed breath of a cloud.
I looked up.
The pale blue morning sky above me
Was full of immeasurable freedom.

4

When I was having lunch
In the Symington Lunchroom,
A young man came in,
Put a nickel
In the juke-box,
And smoking his cigarette
He listened:
"I went to your wedding. . . ."
He played the song just for himself.
His eyes were seeing
Whatever it is sad eyes see.
I listened while I ate,
Thinking. . . and thinking. . . .
I wanted to say to him:
That too is past, my friend.
But here one doesn't say such things.
Then he went out again.

Toronto

I couldn't earn my bread
Sitting at a desk in peace and quiet
Writing of things that weren't true
And that no-one wanted.
And so, to escape my dishonour
As a writer
I worked in a chocolate factory,
And my sweat
Dripped on the sweets
For Canadian children.
Sometimes in the morning, when I was still fresh,
I looked out through the open window
Across Lake Ontario,
Magnificent as new silver in the young light;
Later in the day I'd stop doing that.
In the evening I stepped out of the factory exhausted
And drank the air like clear water.
At night, for one wild moment
My dreams woke up,
But my right hand hurt
And I went to sleep again.
That was my life in Toronto (Ontario), Canada,
And I thought it was good.

This City Like Any Other

1

Years ago, when I came to this big city
All I knew was its name, the rest was alien.
I only knew its location on a big continent.
When does the city where you live become your home?
When you have loved there and said farewell,
And when you stay although you know the living there are dead.

2

When does a city become familiar? I ask myself.
There are other things a guest does not experience
(How could he? He comes, he looks, and goes away again):
To walk the streets all day without anyone looking at you
Let alone talking to you, and thus without uttering a word;
My joy to be alive wore as thin as the soles of my shoes.
You must experience what it's like to live, yes, but live without answers.
And then, years later, you remember: I stood there, the wind
Blew right through me, here at this intersection, yearning for a woman.

3

How rapidly a city grows, how it races on—but where?
Is there no-one who has any idea where our big cities are going?
A few days ago I saw the house where I lived
In the attic—or rather, I didn't see it: it had vanished
Without trace, as if there had never been a single door.
But in the spring light I saw the shadow of a room outlined in the air,
The table a shadow at which we sat, and the bed a shadow
In which two shadows warmed each other who had nothing but themselves.
(How much that was and meant in that first year!) I cannot forget
The summer wind from the open window playing with your hair.
Like all the other things, is it a shadow wind?
Like all that's been, is this but shadow hair?

4
This city, like any other, will never know
That I was here, that I am gone; it doesn't care.
And yet I wish it luck and that its luck may last—
I underline *last*, because the city's loud voice frightens me.
Experience taught us all that cities too can die,
Quickly, unexpectedly—or have we forgotten already? It's but a few years
ago.
They die, and nothing is left of them but smoke to indicate
That there, for God's sake, stood a big city;
Now there is only the surging emptiness of light.
That's why you have to wish this city luck, like a friend you found.
I wish this city, that never knew me and yet was home to me, a long life.

5
When I wake up the city is already there.
I hear its voice; it comes in like a distant surf.
On this sea today some will reach their destinations,
Others, whom God and luck forsook, never will,
However much they try to get a grip on fortune;
They're lucky if they earn their daily bread.
And I? Shivering, I stand at the window. Look—paling quickly,
the morning star!

Dishwashers

1 There's five of us

There's five of us:
Mac, Arthur, Richard, Franco, Walter—
A global mixture, put together from all sorts of places:
Our names, that's all
We know of each other.
We're five dishwashers
From 6 to 3,
Whoever cleans out the kitchen stove stays till 4.
Then we disappear like night-birds
Retiring to their nests.
Don't ask us about "the dignity of work"—
It consists of 28 dollars a week
And free supper.
The dignity is inside me, I'm invulnerable.

2 Mac

Heaven knows what his real name was,
Because there are no Macs in Switzerland,
But that's what they call him here, God knows why.
He was the dishwashers' foreman,
The one who had all the responsibility,
The right hand, so he thought, of the owner
Whom we never saw.
Shining plates were his bliss,
And sparkling glass his triumph;
A broken champagne glass grieved him.
He smoked cigars
And the stumps lay crushed on the plates.
He surveyed the cleaned-up kitchen like a general,
And he gave me orders—me, his slave, who laughed at him inside.
Before he left, at 4 AM, he looked around with satisfaction:
The kitchen sparkled, the pots and pans were waiting for the new day.
Then he went home, suddenly an old man, lonely, frightened.
I would've liked to ask him:
"Mac, how d'you feel? How d'you live?"
I never asked, and he wouldn't have answered.
Mac, how d'you feel? How d'you live? What d'you do
When you're alone?

3 Richard

A small, older man with a meticulous parting of the hair,
Who hadn't lost his formal ways of politeness
And who scrubbed pots and pans as eagerly
As if he were personally responsible for them.
Born in one of those Baltic states now so far away,
He was a Russian soldier in one and a German soldier in the other
world war—
One changes sides when the really big storms blow up
Just in order to survive; he had survived.
Anyway, who could've harmed a little old man
Who would've parted his hair meticulously even in the face of a firing-squad
And then would've said politely: "I'm ready now. Please go ahead."
And didn't he have to try and slip through between the millstones
Which the big powers moved? Is that not what everybody
Has always tried to do—or at least the majority?
Millions were crushed—not he.
He ended up in Germany as a sexton in a church, a polite helper of God,
Worried from the beginning over the behaviour of his children.
Now he was here scrubbing pots and pans
And getting angry when they were burnt inside—"plain negligence on the
part of the cooks!"
During the day, as he told me confidentially, he went from store to store
With heavy boxes full of baking powder—an innocent German product,
The kind that soon after Auschwitz was in demand again everywhere.
He dreamt of huge turnovers
While his wife painted flowers at home,
Dreams for fifteen cents or for one dollar or for a million—
What's the difference?
What kind of dreams do I have?
Better ones than Richard between the millstones?
And where do I live?

4 Franco

Taranto,
In the heel of the Italian boot—
It sounds almost like Toronto,
Except that it's colder here.
Over there the sun blazes with a white light—
Could it melt away poverty and filth?
Once upon a time Greek ships sailed there
On the violet-blue sea—
Did they bring him bread?
There were masses of history in the ground—
What use were they to him?
Can two thousand years of glory
Feed the living?
Taranto meant for him: hardly any work and no prospects.
Canada sounded like: you'll have everything.
Sometimes he sang with a wild voice songs
That conjured up Africa,
And between the knives and forks that he cleaned
He was like a Saracen
Handling weapons gathered after the battle.
Sometimes he spoke to me of wine, spaghetti and cheese.
He was saving up penny by penny
So that his wife and children could join him.
Then his life would be complete again.
A life complete in his way—that's all he wanted.

5 Arthur

Never wrote a line
And yet he had the face of an old sage
Who thought about everything and was familiar with secrets
That we don't know.
Never travelled about the world, always here,
And yet the years had left their mark in the now weary lines of his face.

Look at these trenches filled with shadows
And the lines like rifts of frost that crack the earth.
He hardly talks.
What would he be thinking about when he puts plates and dishes
Into the machine like dirty suns
From 6 to 3?

Only sometimes, when Franco sings with his shrill voice,
He turns around—he works in a corner—
And says, "Shut up!"
That's all. With a calm voice.
Perhaps that too is a kind of epitome of wisdom.

And when the dishwashers' night ends and he has changed,
Where does the old gentleman in the dark coat and with the grey hat go?
To a rendezvous with unknown stars?
To some work he's writing which we'll never read?
To some house where a butler waits and says politely: "Sir. . . ." ?

Or simply to sleep till the following night
When the plates clatter again
And Franco sings?
He goes home to sleep, an old man
Who has not much left,
Just enough to live.

Lonely

Lonely
As the moon
Over the fastest growing
City in the world.
Lonely
As the Northern Lights
Over Hudson Bay
That play for God the silent music
Of their radiance.

Lonely as I
Saturday afternoons
Walking down Yonge Street in Toronto—
An immigrant, a drop
The earth doesn't absorb.
Lonely as I
Sipping a whisky
In the "Western Tavern"
Where I listen to the song of an aging girl
Who sings in order to live.

Toronto Means Meeting-place

Toronto means meeting-place,
It's derived from an Indian word.
Here I met myself
When I was looking for myself as for a stranger.
Here, searching patiently, in discreet passion
I found the seed of joy
And picked it up to make it grow.
Here I reconciled myself
To my own existence, that fleeting shadow,
This brief, bitter-glorious time on earth.
Here I encountered myself
And had long conversations with myself,
Here I changed not only my habits
But I learnt more than just a new *langua*ge.
Here I steeled my No,
Here I heated my Yes to a blaze.

To a Negro

To a negro
Who came toward me in the street:
Forgive me your persecutions everywhere,
Forgive me that you can't find living quarters in white areas.
I said nothing.
He walked past me.

To an old Jew
Who glanced at me:
Forgive me your extermination in Germany,
Forgive me the ovens, the death marches, the graves.
I said nothing.
He walked past me.

To an old woman
Wearing a rustic kerchief:
Forgive me your expulsion and flight
From Hungary, Romania, and everywhere else,
Forgive me the cold refugee sky here.
I said nothing.
She walked past me.

To one
Who came to meet me:
I forgive you nothing.
To one who would say nothing
And whom I recognized:
Nothing will be forgiven you.
I said that to myself.

Curriculum Vitae I

Revolutions
Had driven him from one country to another.
Too often he'd put down roots in alien ground
And thought that at last he could stay.
But storms, of which he was innocent,
Came and drove him away again
And finally across the sea.
His home was in Saporoshje
But he had no peace there.
Only his face was still
Earth from Russian earth,
And when he walked, slowly, deliberately
(Even when work had to be done in a hurry),
He looked as if he were walking
Across a summer field in the Ukraine.
But Gregory had turned into George.

Curriculum Vitae II

He was Greek
And came from a small village in the Peleponnesus.
Thirty years ago
He heard the word "Canada"
And that'd carried him away from the Aegean Sea.
It'd sounded so big,
As if there were vast lands to be had
And many got them too—
But not he.
Since then he's worked in a factory
And has made enough to support wife and children.
Perhaps his name was once Ulysses,
He doesn't talk about that,
Here he's Bill.
His children, born on Canadian soil,
know nothing of Telemachus,
Or Penelope who wove the veil of expectation,
And they prefer
The swaying of the maples in an Indian summer
To the hard light on Attic marble
That feeds no-one.

The Old Woman

The old woman with the kerchief of Slavic peasants
Got on the streetcar and said haltingly
And with a foreign accent, the name of a street.
She didn't belong here, perhaps she'd just arrived
And this was her first excursion. Now she knew
That she would arrive at her destination,
And the conductor said cheerfully:
"Sure, old lady, we'll take you there."
Calmly she sat down, there was no embarrassment, no shame,
She sat down as if on the wicker chair by the stove after a long day's work,
And she looked out with tranquillity as if she were looking across fields.
Kerchief and pleated skirt. Her hands like brown, now crumbling earth
    in her wide lap,
And in her face the years of her village.
She carried everything with her: the summer wind, stillness,
The stillness of an unbroken world through which time flows as it should.
I saw her get up and then—she seemed to grow and look beyond us—
Out in the street she walked slowly as if she had plenty of time
And as if there were still the ploughed fields in the spring wind,
An old woman with the kerchief of Slavic peasants,
An old mother of the earth.

Wind and Rain

How soft the night wind is
In the maple outside my window,
17 Madison Avenue, Toronto.
Did it move differently in the copper beech
Outside the window where I used to live?

How much it rains in these November days,
And the earth, expecting winter,
Answers with silence.
Does it rain like that only here?
In what language does the earth answer the rain
Over there where I used to live?

Emigrant

He lives now
On a huge new continent,
But he pines away
For a country that
No longer exists.
His letters to history
Are returned unanswered;
He collects them carefully
As evidence of his faith.
In the silence of two continents
He grows thin and old.
"Where is my reward?" he whispers.
At last he falls silent, yearning
For a country that no longer exists.
His children shake their heads
About the old man.
They're doing fine.

I Confess

I confess
That my eyes sometimes
Search the sky for messages
(Is spring coming soon. . . ? Or going further:
Why am I here? What's the meaning of it all?)
But always and very quickly they return to earth.
When I see the long line-up of men
Outside the Scott Mission waiting for food
I abandon my excursions into the blue
Or to the moon
Or into myself.
There's still lots waiting to be done around here.

In the City

1

In the huge apartment building
Across from my own
Most of the windows
Are dark tonight.
It's Friday and people are out.
But I notice somebody
In one of the few windows
In which there is light.
Is he looking across at mine?
How big the city is tonight.

2

At night in the window
My mirror image.
Whose is that familiar face?
Who is the curious stranger?
That transparent figure, sitting in the night,
Traversed by floating lights—
Who is he?

Who is it that follows
Every one of my movements,
Wears my things, whose hand
Moves exactly like mine
Across an identical sheet of paper?
I've known him
For more than half a century,
The fugitive stranger,
My dear friend.
Who is he?

3

Think:
In the course of this night
The leaves will grow.
And the blossoms on the ground
Will open a little more.
While I sleep is something inside me
Growing too?

Canada

At all times long rows of cars
Guided with precision by lights,
The herds of waiting cars on parking lots
Or at their watering places, the gas stations—
Apart from an occasional accident,
Duly reported, with photographs, in the *Daily Star*—
What self-assurance of life!
How rapidly things move here into the future!
Not far from the cities
Endless forests breathe
As on the first day of the world,
And further north,
Above Hudson Bay and regions that never wake up—
While down here cars, twin-eyed,
Carve up the night—
Northern Lights
Moving gigantically in flaming silence
Converse about nothing.

Lesson from the Arctic

Some people I know
who have lived in the arctic
tell me
that up there in the ice
and what with the continuous effort
just to breathe
you become aware of the earth.
One of them, I was told,
after his return from up north,
could not tear himself away
from the sight of a flowershop.
Others assured me that there
where there is nothing
and where nothing is easy
they found an enchantment
of almost unbearable grandeur.
All of them yearned
to return to the arctic.
But I took the lesson to heart—
of the man who succumbed
on his return
to the enchantment of flowers.

Interview with an Older Man

1
When he was asked
Whom he had loved most,
He was silent; but they could see
That he was thinking of all those
He had embraced.

"Be silent and give away no-one!"
He said. "I read that
In a book when I was young,
Before I ever learned to love."

2
Later on, adding to this, he said:
"The torso of Aphrodite
In the Museo Nazionale in Naples
Was precious to me.
I saw it once only,
In my youth.
I loved Aphrodite—
But she didn't respond.
She's still there;
She'll not die with me."

3
What else he loved they wanted to know.
"Flowers," he answered, "and blossoms."
Why?
"They're silent. They simply bloom.
They pass quickly.
Poppies in the fields. Roses.
Tulips. Forsythias coming out
To greet spring.
The first blossoms especially—
Winter's hard
Not only on people getting old."

4
What else?
"My fellow-men," he said simply.
"What would I do here without them?"
And he added: "Certain contemporaries
I make a point of avoiding."

5
Which flag
And what colour
Did he like best?
"White," he answered,
"Because it contains all the other colours.
And white is the space
Into which the future
Can be written.
Once I loved red
More than the rest,
But now it's white.
I'd also like to mention blue,
The colour
Of the African violet
On my window-sill,
The colour of a gentle salute
That greeted me so often
With unexpected cheer."

6
What did he think
Of today's young people
Who were in evidence everywhere now
And who condemned everything (including him)?
"It's difficult for them to be young,
But they too will grow older, I hope,"
He answered. "They're no better
Than my friends.
They'll be worse if they don't
Break out of their prisons."

"They too won't be able to manage," he added,
"Without the old virtues."

7
Did losses
Still hurt him?
And which ones?

(He'd lost many things
Because of the times he lived in.
He could've filled a whole notebook
Called "Losses").

"The loss of my eyes
With which to see the light
The loss of my heart
With which to be moved.
The loss of laughter."

8
Was it true that he still hated?
"Yes."
Couldn't he be reconciled with everyone?
"No."
So he didn't expect to be on good terms with everyone?
"Not at all."

9
What did he think about, they asked,
When he lay awake at night?

"That this night could be my last one
That the morning of the new day
Could be my last one.
I think of my father and mother,
Long dead but still alive in me, immortal
Until I die.
Of my brothers and sisters, still living.
Of my friends, dead and alive, here and there.
Sometimes of some young man or woman,
Unknown to me, who
Some day may read what I've written
And think: I would've liked to know that man,
Perhaps we would've been friends.
I'm his friend already, and I rely on him.
Or I simply think that I lie here
In a bed that doesn't belong to me
On Roxborough Street East,
Toronto, Ontario,
Canada
On the North American continent,
In this world,
Under a sky that encompasses all,
And I feel the mystery
And it overwhelms me.
I think of my being here
And that it is still very good."

10
Was he melancholic
At times?

"Melancholy is the salt
That comes with my bread.
It serves to make
The morning star brighter.
Good things receive from it
More light."

11

What did he think of God,
If that question was permitted?

Then he told them
The old Jewish legend of the Rabbi
In a tiny village in Poland
Who went into the synagogue one night,
Making his round as usual,
And there, in a dark corner,
Sat God.
The Rabbi prostrated himself and called out:
"Lord, what are You doing here?" And God replied,
Not with thunder and storm, but
With a faint voice:
"I'm tired, Rabbi, I'm tired to death."

But what did that have to do with him?
"I don't want to make Him even more tired.
He's carrying burdens enough."

12

Was there one nation
He loved especially?
(And he saw in their eyes a flag, but
He couldn't make out the colours.)

"I love people," he said.

"Yes," he added, "I love
My unhappy nation, the more unhappy
It becomes in its glutted fortunes the more
Attached I am to it. But as I said,
I love people."

How was it
That he didn't prefer a particular nation?

"Because of my fatherland," he answered.

But wasn't he a German, after all?

"To my last day
I'll have been made from German clay.
The question is
What's been added to the clay?"

13

Was there anything he regretted?

"Yes. To have hurt many people
More deeply than I'd intended to."

"To have been cowardly
When I should've been courageous."

"To have survived
When so many died and so many better ones."

"To have trembled with fear
When I should've been fearless."

"To have crawled
When I should've walked upright."

"That my shadow
Often grew too heavy for me
Because I was a German in my time."

"Not to have done anything better.
Not to have been more joyful.
Not to have been more magnanimous.
Yes, not enough magnanimity—there's
Too little of it in the world."

"But I'm still alive. Still learning."

14
Was there a language
He was especially fond of?

"Yes. The language of my childhood.
The language of the sources deep inside me,
Deep in the earth of centuries.
The language of my parents and
Of my first love and many thereafter.
The language of my old friends.
The language that flows in me like blood,
Breathes, laughs, laments,
The language that was scourged in my time.
The language in which the brook's waters ran.
The language in which the first springs came.
The language in which the men of the twentieth of July
Nineteenhundredandfortyfour
Defended the dignity of man.
The language in which Mildred Harnack cried out
Before her execution: And yet I love Germany!

Yes. And the language of my later and last years,
That taught me fresh ways to say things.
The language that received me as a guest and treated me royally,
Gave me bread and water and other good things.
The language in which I speak to my students,
To friends, to strangers.
The language that generously allowed me
To be at home in it
As guest, as immigrant, as friend of the world."

15
So then he didn't feel
Uprooted?

"Are my roots
Not in the earth
Wherever I am?

My roots
are in the earth."

16
What, they wanted to know
Finally, did he think of mankind?
Surely, after all
That had happened, not much?

"There's still much ahead of us."

Did that mean
He really held out
Hope for man?

"Not hope.
Certainty."

17
How would he
Sum up
His life?

"I was here."

Anything else?

Then his voice grew strong
And there was
Agony and triumph
In a single sentence:

"I was here.
It was good to be here."

18
Did he have any message
For his friends, known
And unknown?

"S'en aller! S'en aller!
La parole de vivant!"

Onward!
The charge of the living!

Sentimental Journeys

I would like to revisit
The temple at Paestum
And Brueghel's "Parable of the Blind" in Naples.
I would like to sit again
In the cathedral of Chartres
And in the golden stillness
Of San Marco in Venice.
Is that really what I want? One should
Avoid sentimental reunions.
I would sooner drift on the Yukon
Toward the light of the arctic
Trembling
In the freshness of the icy void.

II

Brueghel: 'The Parable of the Blind'

The passage of six blind beggars across the canvas—
A downward motion, a falling down nothing can stop:
The blind following the blind inevitably fall.
So much for the picture. A testament. Such famous last words
Are recorded and signed at the end, not at the beginning.
Soon afterward he died. 1569. Companion in his time
Of Rabelais, Montaigne, Shakespeare: seers, like him.
Caught in an obscurity between old and new
Time gnashes its teeth and fearfully, hungrily
Demands the unknown. Before the painting of the beggars
There were other pictures—the whole Brueghel
Inventory of Flanders and the world.

Icarus fell and no-one saw it;
Not a speck to stain the bright day.
The Tower of Babel grows as trees grow
Into the sky; except that nature sees to it that they don't.
The crucifixion looks like a public festival, not just anywhere,
But in Flanders; and he who dies is ignored.
Likewise the Massacre of the Innocents, the census in Augustus' time—
All taking place on the rich and fertile ground of Flanders,
On Brueghel's own ground: if there are hills and mountains,
The artist moved them, playing creator *à la mode.*
Here the seasons pass through their time of year,
Fruit is harvested, the golden skin of grain is flayed,
At noon the mowers stretch out in the shadow of a tree.
November brings home the cows' pasture; hunter and hounds
Return to the fires of the hearth; a winter's day for children
Becomes an icy spring, the river a crunching frozen track.
The peasants at their roaring dance, benches buckle
And belts are undone amid gorging, smacking, belching, lust.

Such is the world. A good world. Today
Lies between yesterday and what's to come, even though
The sky is black and Spanish, and heads are rolling
(Egmont, Horn). All is folly, all vanity, for
All is life, like a children's game, serious, without laughter,
Proverbs everyone lives by though he sees through them—
To be undeceived is not enough: caught together, hanged together.
The gluttons lie idly in a land of plenty: Cockaigne.
"Mad Griet" and her troop of women are not afraid
To plunder hell itself; poor devils, soundly thrashed;
Rabid greed knows but excess. Then comes death,
Hordes of deaths: decrepitude, cadavers, putrefaction—black triumph
That levels all. Call that "the harvest."
All this is Brueghel's inventory of Flanders and the world.

And then, on a lovely day in lovely Flanders,
The sky a soft blue of gentle light, the earth at rest,
So still you could hear the thud of a fruit falling to the ground—
There they come, six beggars, blind, led by one who has no eyes.
This day like every other, they trust him blindly
And in the same way trust each other, and the hand
They put on the unseen shoulder of the man in front,
Felt but never looked upon, is their link to warmth and security.
They rely on the file-leader, his darkness still knows distance.
Warmth means: village. Wind is: open spaces. Rain means:
Defencelessness. Snow: all is still and cold. Yet they trust him
As if they saw what he doesn't see. He can't see. Suddenly he trips.
Wetness means: brook. But he falls deeper. That's where it starts.

The suction starts. The second has lost his balance on the staff,
Trips over him and pulls down by his stick the third
Who does not know yet, is straining to know: something
Is wrong, but what?—How easy things are for those who see!
His hand on the shoulder of the third, the fourth stops,
Hesitates and thinks: there is a motion that draws him on—O he would
Pop the empty eyes out of his head to see, if he could!
Then all would be fine. It's the same for the last two, the fifth and the sixth,
Still in good hands, at ease (almost), the message
Has not reached them yet: they too are meant to fall.
From the first to the last the wave rolls on,
From the last to the first it comes out of the dark.
All this in stillness and on a lovely day, the earth at peace,
And who walks in the light and sees it, he is rich
(Although one wonders if those with sight see more).
So still, you could hear the thud of a fruit falling to the ground.
But the blind beggars' fall does nothing to disrupt the day.
The earth is blind and deaf. If not, she watches unconcerned
As the blind must fall when led by the blind.
Patience! They'll struggle to their feet again after the fall,
They'll recover, dust themselves off and walk on in darkness.

Faces

1
The other day
I saw faces
Of men and women
So utterly bleak, so empty
That I said compassionately:
My poor friends.
They were frozen with terrible fear
And absolutely empty.
Had they lost their children,
Their beloved, their relatives,
In an accident, the sort
Our papers are full of,
And had the news just reached them?
Or perhaps they'd witnessed
With their own eyes
The dying of a stranger,
And that was why
Their faces were so overcome
With horror?
Or had they realized
Finally, at that very moment,
That the giant mushroom clouds
Would no longer shoot up for experiments only,
In other words, did they know
That they themselves would die—soon?
Worse things had happened to them:
They'd witnessed,
Frozen with fear,
With petrified faces,
The unexpected rise and fall
Of the stock-market:
They'd lost their money—quite
Suddenly, like
Snapping your fingers—gone.
They'd lost what was most precious to them,
What their hearts treasured,
Lost, lost. It was terrible,
It was worse than losing
Wife, child, father, mother, job, land,

Worse than losing faith (did I say "faith"?),
Losing truth,
Much worse than losing the message
From the Mount of Olives,
The Ten Commandments,
It was worse than losing everything,
Absolutely everything—
They'd lost their money, yes, that was it:
The stock-market had crashed, unexpectedly—
And they'd been so sure, much surer
Than they were of immortality (because what's immortality
Without money?)
Yes, that was it: they'd lost their money.
They'd staked their money
And lost. It'd been
A poor bet and they lost all.
I walked away indifferently.
I remembered other faces.

2

I remembered
Other faces.
I remembered
The face of my mother
When she got the news
That her son had died in battle
For the Fatherland
(Naturally—for what else should he have died?)
Her face was white and empty, drained
Of everything, she'd lost something
That could never be replaced. Never.
I remembered that when I saw
These empty faces,
Empty with fear, petrified
Because they'd lost their money.
They desecrated my mother's face.

3

I have seen
The face of hunger.
There's nothing to add to that.
Hunger has no colour:
It's simply hunger.
Hunger has no faith:
It's simply hunger.
Hunger has no hope
Except to be stilled.
Hunger has no history,
No dignity, no trust.
I have seen
The face of hunger.
There's nothing to add to that.
O God—yes, they who'd
Lost everything, absolutely everything,
They desecrated even the face of hunger.

4

I have seen
The face of a little boy.
He was standing in a garden
Before a blossom.
What did he see? What was he looking at
So intently, so completely absorbed?
Did he see the blossom only? There was nothing
In the world between him and
This tiny red sun.
His child's face was filled
With wonder, with magic, with life.
Did they who lost their money
Never know about that?
They've buried everything
And their tombstone reads:
They're dead. They lost their money.
They're dead, dead, dead.
No resurrection for them. No reawakening.
On that last and first day
(As the story goes)
What is going to be given to them?
Blank cheque-books: toys
For an infinitely empty eternity.

5

I remember
Other faces.
I remember
The face of a dead friend.
His silence was the sum of all life.
Most delicate dwelling, now deserted or
Perhaps not deserted, perhaps
Inhabited even in its decay
By a very soft, inexplicable scent
Composed of who he really was.
There I stood at the edge
Of a continent
That I could not discover
Until my hour came.
Most living, most delicate stone.
But the faces here were
Dead stone. Inhabited by fear.
Dead.

6

I have seen the faces
Of those who were led
Out of the flames
Of the Warsaw ghetto
To their execution,
Carried out according to
The latest scientific methods
Or quite simply
By wholesale disposal,
As they say in business.
To this should be added:
Nothing.
Except: shame.
Except—no, nothing.
And these here
Had lost their money.

7
I have seen
Faces and faces,
But never any like these, so empty,
So overcome with horror,
They'd lost everything,
They'd lost their money.
I've read in faces
The story of human passions
And I trembled.
I've seen
My own face
Like a moon, half light, half shade,
Unknown to me,
My own face like that
Of a cherished but distant stranger.
Divine clay,
Shot through with a soft beam of light.
But no faces like these here.

8
They had forgotten.
They'd forgotten all
The good things of life.
Sleep. Bread. Love.
The seasons.
They didn't remember anymore,
They'd forgotten.
They'd lost their money.
They'd also forgotten that here
Everything is insecure.
They wanted to erect an idol,
Something perfect and infallible,
Guaranteeing safety:
Security.
Now there was nothing left—Oh horrible:
Nothing. Nothing. Nothing.
Empty. Lost.
They'd lost their money.
They desecrated themselves.

9

Yet another face
Came back to me,
The face of a man
Who many years ago (Or is it
That since July nineteenhundredandfortyfour
Not years have passed but
A whole eternity? Don't trouble the memory!)
Now, then, he died.
This man was
Sentenced to death
By Hitler's henchmen
Judges,
And I remember his face
When he was told, when they
Yelled at him that he would die,
That they would hang him (he didn't know
It would be from a meat-hook).
How calm his face looked all of a sudden!
His silence was radiant.
It was the face of an ultimate dignity.
It was the face of inviolable hope.
It was the face of humanity.
He would die, he knew that and
That wasn't easy; but he died
For something: perhaps one could say
For the deliverance of man
From chaos.
Yes, and those others'd lost their money.
They froze with fear. They turned
To stone, empty, quite empty.
They desecrated the face of the man
Who died for them.

10

Take a good look at these faces.
Look into their frozen hearts.
Look at their terrible fear,
Their petrified horror.
They've lost everything:
They've lost their money.

Leave them alone
In their sorrow.
Do not
Console them.

A Long Journey

"I haven't seen you
In a long time. . ."

I've just come
Back from faraway lands.

"Where've you been, traveller?"

In the history
Of my people.

"One should return rested
From the trips one takes."

Not from this one.
From this one never.

"I can see it
In your face. You had
Sleepless nights and
Strenuous days, traveller."

Too many.
Too many. And I was alone.

"But sleepless nights—why?
What did you see, traveller?"

I saw too much.
I saw too much misery.
I saw too much blindness.
I saw too much pride.
I saw too much acquiescence.
I saw too much treachery.
I saw too much palliation.
I saw—

"Nothing else? Nothing
A little brighter, traveller?"

I saw goodwill: not enough.
I saw sacrifices: in vain.
I saw noble people exiled.
I saw the execution of the brave.
I saw resistance: overrun
And forgotten.
I saw the extinction of peoples.
I saw—
My heart broke from what I saw.

"Enough.
What did you hear, traveller?"

I heard the triumph
When they were victorious.
I heard the lamentations
When they were defeated.
I heard the cries of enthusiasm.
I heard feet march
Across whole countries.
I heard the moaning in camps,
I heard the stillness there, more terrible than screams.
I heard complacent self-praise.
I heard—

"Enough.
What landscapes did you visit,
Traveller?"

Belgium, France, Holland, Denmark,
Norway, Yugoslavia, Greece, Italy,
Russia, Czechoslovakia—in some of them
I spent a lot of time.

"Too much for one trip, my friend.
Why not save something
For another journey, traveller?"

They are the countries to which
German history took me.
One country I forgot.

"Which one, traveller?"

Germany.

"Why Germany, traveller?"

That's where it started, and
That's where it ended.

"What ended, traveller?"

The dream. The blindness.
The arrogance. The hubris.

"And what places did you find
Most unforgettable?"

Verdun. Ypres. The Somme. Flanders.
Stalingrad.

"Nothing to admire there,
Traveller?"

Nothing to admire. But lots
To lament—the dead, all
Victims of hubris.

"You're weary, traveller."

I'm not weary. It's just
That my heart broke.

"You've been travelling for too long,
Traveller."

Not for long enough.

"You need sleep, traveller."

To dream of my journey?
There are other places that
Do not let me sleep.

"Tell me which they are, traveller."

Buchenwald. Auschwitz. Theresienstadt.
Warsaw. And so forth.
And so forth.

"Not a pleasant trip, traveller.
Why didn't you go to picturesque Switzerland,
Especially the Tessin?
Why not to Spain, to the
Costa Brava, above all?
Or why not, for instance, to Ireland?
Close your eyes and enjoy yourself?
In any case, why
Take such a depressing journey at all?"

I wanted to know.
For the last time I wanted to know.

"What did you want to know, traveller?"

That I am a German—
That's what I wanted to know.
So as to find a way
Out of my prison.
So as not to die
From my knowledge.

"Take a rest, traveller,
You need sleep."

I would like to rest
Because I need sleep.
But I cannot sleep
Because I sorrow.

"But time
Has gone on, traveller."

Has it?

"And your travels into the past
Were superfluous, traveller."

Perhaps. But not for me:
Now I know, and knowledge
Excludes forgetting.
And I want to tell the story
Of my travels
To those who don't know
Because they were blessed with youth:
My friends, the young ones—

"O traveller—you rash, foolish
Dreamer of useless dreams,
D'you think they want
To hear any of this?"

I leave that to them.
Of one's travels
One must tell.

New Dictionary

America too
Now has its own
Dictionary of inhumanity.
Escalation, napalm, interrogation,
Defoliation, body-count, saturation bombing
Are some of the unforgettable entries.
However, the German original
Distinguishes itself by a
Precise and pedantic methodology
And is, even if forgotten,
Still unsurpassed.
Language too can receive
Wounds that never heal.

An American Travelogue

I travelled to Frankfurt
And came to Detroit, USA.
I went to West Berlin
And found myself in Houston, Texas.
I spent some time in Milan
And they went for my dollars
Like the sharks of Chicago.
O but they've learnt,
They're smart cookies.
And of course they're all
Anti-American.

Kinship

Quite a few Americans
Experience now
What so many Germans
Experienced during the Nazi years:
Suffering. Not to wish
Their own country well,
To know that what is happening
Has to end badly because
It is built on the sandhill of hubris,
To watch the name of their country
And thus their own name being tarnished.
My sympathies to them.
My friends and I, all older people now,
We know.

Guernica: Vague Memories

Some of the older men, who live peacefully with their families now,
Secure in their professions, earning a decent salary,
Their children grown up (some of them probably at university),
And who after a full working life will be pensioned off in a few years' time
So they can enjoy a peaceful old age, if the tenuous peace holds—
In 1936, that is to say centuries ago,
They volunteered to go to Spain as members of the *Legion Condor*
To assist Franco and to strangle the Republic.

At that time—centuries ago, measured by memory—
They were well fed, strapping, blond young men
Who, without giving it a thought, bombarded Guernica,
Filled as they were with the idea of the *Führer* (if you still remember)—
Guernica, what is Guernica?—Hecuba, what is Hecuba?

In the evenings now they listen to records of Bach,
Played by Pablo Casals, an old man from Spain
("Incomparable, don't you think?"—"Very... very beautiful."—"Sublime.")
Who, after the fall of the Republic, never again stepped on Spanish soil.

Their children admire Picasso's "Guernica"
("Magnificent"—"Moving"—"The whole terror of our time.")
But their fathers who, like everyone else, earned the right to a peaceful
 old age,
Destroyed Guernica and the Republic.
As I say, that was centuries ago.

Pablo Casals grew old and died.
Picasso grew old and died.
Those who bombarded Guernica have grown old. Some of them too have
 died.
And the young admire Picasso's "Guernica," of course only
From a purely artistic point of view. "Because," they say,
"What have we got to do with Guernica?" If it comes to that, what was
 Guernica?

Political Emigrant

He who runs away excludes himself from history,
Though he may regard himself as the champion of the hopes of many;
He likes to hear the footfall of a thousand fleeing refugees—
If he had read his history he would know better than that.

He goes away, and those he used to lead are left with a shrug
To accommodate to new conditions in their old house as best they can;
The living want to survive: existence precedes consciousness.
O the illusions he resurrects each day in order to go on living.

Expectations, nurtured with care, to preserve a *raison d'être*,
The hope that. . . But it does not bear fruit,
Because in foreign lands such hope crumbles like old bread,
And what he says, his pleas and protests, others do not understand.

Pity becomes politeness, and deaf ears are soon strained.
He plays at liberation on an empty stage and just for himself,
And soon no dog will cock an ear to listen to his sorrows.
He who was somebody has become a nobody and can't believe it.

In waiting for what never comes, his hair turns grey.
The young take over: "He? Who? When?" And: "Unknown here."
His country of origin is never expunged from his passport—emigrant
  forever.
History doesn't laugh at or regret anything: it simply goes on.
The old sower with his dried-up seed—where is he? Vanished. Gone.

Goya: House of a Deaf Man

Quinta del Sordo—that's what the neighbours call it.
The house is home to one who is deaf.
Goya hears no more. Once he wrote on a piece of paper:
"I have seen." He saw—everything from beginning to end.
After that, what need is there of ears?
The voice of Rosarito, little daughter of his housekeeper
(Occasionally his bed-companion) would be sweet to hear;
He cannot hear it. But when they walk in the garden
Or in the streets, he can feel the budding warmth
Of her little hand in his; it comforts him.
At 75 what is there apart from painting?
Besides, he not only saw, he *lived*: wife, children, the Duchess
Of Alba (a little eccentric, charming and good in bed,
But better still on canvas: Maja naked and clothed).

So then he's deaf and has accepted it, because he knows
All the voices between tiny Fuentetodos and Madrid
And Rome, way back into what were later called "dark times."
He heard. He lived. And he survived. You live as a matter of course,
But to survive requires wisdom, and wisdom is a handmaid—
Does she not bend her back in polite silence? The willow
Bends thus with the wind; that way it doesn't break, and the storm passes.
Lords and masters change, but the times remain dark. That's why
He painted the oppressor and the liberator and the same old new aristocrats:
Luisa, Carlo, the upstart Godoy and Joseph Bonaparte, as well as
Wellington, the victor (*"Y viva Velinton!"* And soon thereafter—
"Long live Ferdinand! Long live our chains!" You must understand
The people: they carry their burdens, they die, they welcome fetters,
Shake them off and pick up their burdens again)—
The list reads like *Who's Who?* in Spain. Long ago, when he left home,
His wise mother gave him a notebook in which she had entered
The names and ancestries of the best families: "You'll need them."
The notebook is brimful and every name is a picture signed "Goya."
Those who live carefree and easy in the light have their portrait painted.

Goya, they say, changed with the wind. He learnt from the willows.
He bent, but not merely for the sake of his mother's notebook.
There were sketchbooks: *Proverbios*, *Caprichos*, *Los Desastros de la Guerra*,
A whole world of horror, incurable and absurd, without names, but
With inscriptions: "Bury them and be silent", "Why?", "Cure impossible,"
And "I have seen," "The Mamelukes" and "The third of May": the man
in the white shirt
Flaming like a torch held high before being cast into the night.
That's how revolts die. That's how the people die. What for?
They just die. For new chains and fetters. Look at the picture!
Goya the seer. The painter is an eye, wide open, cold, yet always taking in,
And his hand follows the lines of his sight to allocate light and dark.

Quinta del Sordo—that's what the neighbours call it.
A deaf man lives here, Goya, who hears no more.
But he can still see, and seeing is hearing.
In the silence, already empty as a tomb, he paints—
No longer for Doña X or Joseph Bonaparte or Wellington, but for himself.
What he sees now comes from inside him, rises soundless to the surface
And spreads like a black flood. He is dictating his last will to the bright walls.
A great slurping, smacking and crunching of bones splashes through the
house.
Saturn devours one of his children. Blood juice. It tastes good.
A colossus grows. Panic: nations flee. Witches laugh.
San Isidoro is waiting for his drunken pilgrims. What is it
That creature whispers to the old man leaning on his staff? What is it
The grinning witch is cooking in her pot? The Fates: what are they brewing?
Demons timeless in time. A deaf old man
Covers the walls, fills every space in the house
With what he has seen. His last will: "We never learn anything."
Smacking, slurping and belching echo through the house day and night.
"I have seen." Saturn tears his son to pieces and devours him.

Messages from Victims of War

I

DON'T TALK TO ME ABOUT BIG AND IMPORTANT THINGS
Nor about peace in the world.
You're silent? Don't you believe in them either?
Yes, I see you were one of us—except
That the wave hurled you back on the beach.
I think: our truth is melancholy
With a feeble core of hope.
Don't talk about big and important things.
As far as I am concerned they can go to the moon
Or to Sirius—what difference does it make?
What I want are little things:
Just once more that first day in March
When the brooks begin to run again
And the earth whispers mysteriously—there's only joy,
Quite simply the joy of being alive.
And then in September the fog, like ghosts
Breathing cold into your face—
You shudder... Fall is returning...
The leaves in flames, a fire that doesn't burn.
And then from up in the clouds the hawk's cry,
As if calling to another still far away:
Look, our freedom!
And finally, to watch the evening star rise—
You light upon it suddenly and you're filled with joy,
For beauty always comes upon you gently and unexpectedly.
Those are the things I'd like to experience again.
I'd take such pleasure in them as never before,
Because my eyes have now matured,
My heart knows more.
Where has it all gone?
Lucky those who are still in the light.
But he who lives in the light
Doesn't realize it.

2

I BELIEVED IN GLORY.
To me it was an eagle with golden eyes,
And I thought it would carry me up into the light.
They talked of flags. I believed in flags,
I stormed after them—
And dawn turned into night,
A lasting night—how long already?
This morning children passed by here, and they sang
A song in their own language.
Isn't there something I have forgotten in my life?
I wanted glory, I lapped up its promises,
Now I have plenty of time to think about it,
For this peace will never be broken.
What use were all the medals they gave me,
That I was admired by lesser slaves of glory?
I'd like to run after the children and call:
Sing, o sing for me once more and once again!
Here everything just passes by. Here, there's only silence.
This is glory's tomb.

3

IF I HAD COME BACK—
But I shan't come back.
If I had come back,
I would've proclaimed tidings of a new life,
Because down in the abyss, trapped in a gorge of fire,
I had intimations of another kind of existence—
O everything should be born anew!
I'd come like an ascetic down from the mountains
After a long retreat and shout: Brothers, my brothers!
But I shan't come back, I remain
In the exile of everlasting silence.
What're they doing now, tell me, I yearn to know,
Because the dead—make no mistake about that—
Have a share in your life forever, they're your conscience.
You say they talk and talk and do the same things?
Still the same things they did when we...
In that case it would be better to yearn no more,
But to rest in this deep, cold, never-ending silence.
You say they barter for positions, drown in torrents of words?
Is there nothing then but the past?
O the fools—my brothers!
Don't tell them anything about me. I want to sleep.

4

IT WAS THE SAME WITH ME AS WITH THE OTHERS,
Nothing special at all.
Only thing was that it caught up with me
On a morning, clear and fresh, in France.
I'd always wanted to see Paris;
It's supposed to be very charming, especially the Eiffel Tower,
And I saved up to go there.
Now all I saw were white sheets in a French field hospital,
And my dealings were with death who wanted me.
In the end I gave in, because death wouldn't stop wanting me
As if there were something special about me.
But I was only a petty clerk, not a Field Marshal.
Sometimes I felt a soft hand on my forehead,
And someone said, meaning me, *"pauvre garçon"*—
I knew a little French.
The hand so soft—it told me a lot,
And when at last I gave in, death was so friendly,
Sitting on my bed, showing me many pictures from my youth
And taking me to the top of the Eiffel Tower.
Up there, among the white clouds, I fell asleep.
The hand—if you come across it, give it my thanks.
I'd always wanted to visit France,
I think I would've made friends there.
Now I'm here,
And all the soil of France is my friend.

and my flat in the house of death?
I'm right here! Here—this heap of rubble is my grave.
There are quite a few of us here; I think it's 21.
But we don't bother each other, we're all patience now.
Sometimes the landlord comes and asks how we're doing,
And we answer: "We're dying into ever-increasing decay."
How it all happened I can't tell you—there was simply
A darkness that screamed, and before that
There was a hissing in the air, a star fell from the sky—
I guess God left it to the stars to fall or not to fall,
And one after the other came down, because the stars hate the earth.
I wasn't concerned for myself, but for my child—here it is.
D'you hear how gently it sleeps? I forget—you can't hear that,
You're an outsider.
I brought everything along, even the flowers, the pretty geraniums,
Also the kitchen with all the utensils, and all my clothes.
Strange to think that we're here now, so close to life,
As if we resided by a river. There's such rushing and flowing.
Last night a couple stood in the shadow of the bombed archway
And kissed—it made me yearn for my husband.
Is everything the way it used to be? You say. . .
That we've died in vain—quite forgotten? O God!
Go away, leave us—or I won't be able to endure death any longer,
Or I shall dig myself up through these ruins
And scream
Day and night.
Then, from the force of my screams
God himself will fall down from the stars
And die.

6

UNDER MY TEARS I WAS DELIGHTED WITH THEM

Each time they came,
And always they went away again.
I knew where they went and what was happening there—
Why didn't I keep them home?
Mothers are supposed to be prudent and wise—
But O they're not, they're blind like everyone else.
I handed them over to death, I myself, trembling,
And death took both of them.
Every night, for a long time, he aimed at my heart
And laughed and said, "just a little longer."
My prayers at night were like stones I threw into the sky
That had fallen down on me, and I went on throwing them
For a long time—and then I stopped.
Under my tears I was delighted with them,
But I did nothing about it—does anyone ever?
Suddenly I could bear the silence no longer,
I wanted to be with them, at least in the silence, in death,
Never again to be separated by any farewells.
I looked for them—O mothers are tireless—
And I found them and took them to my breast.
There they lay, my twins, as tiny as they were born.
No-one could've recognized them, they were so disfigured,
But I knew them at once. Don't ask if they're my sons!
They are. Whoever they were: I declare them to be my sons now,
I wipe out the shadows of frontiers,
Mothers don't belong to a country, they belong to the earth,
La mère is the same as *mother*.
Resting now with my sons in this silence
I find my grave too small.
I grow like a tree in fertile soil,
I expand, I embrace everybody,
I say: You, my sons.
I become earth and my sons rest in me as they did in the beginning.
I am boundless earth.

7

EVERYMAN'S MESSAGE:

I could tell you any name
Because I'm everybody,
I was Everyman and I died.
What does it mean to quote the statistics of death?
Millions? A million times Everyman?
And then the women and children.
I was: two hands, two feet, two eyes,
Everything a human being is: flesh and spirit.
I died though I should've lived.
Give everyone alive this message from Everyman here:
Create a human world for man to live in!
In a little while—that's Everyman's message from everywhere—
In just a little while the graves of the dead
Shall be in flames before the eyes of all the living,
And everything will perish in a blaze—O triumph of the idle, forgotten dead!
Nothing will remain.
Death will then be superfluous, he too will die,
And God'll be alone again as at the beginning of time,
Solitary spectator of dawns that give joy to no-one,
Of night skies that will awe no-one.
That, then, will be Everyman's victory. Perhaps,
Perhaps God'll then start all over again the work of creation
That we betrayed,
And at the edge of the cosmos he'll repeat the word
That we forgot.
There'll be no ears left to hear the message,
And there'll be no eyes
To greet the birth of the new light.
Over there the first day will spring from God's hands.
Here there'll be night
Without past, without future.
Light was the first word.
Night—O listen to Everyman's message—
Will night be our last word?

Easy Way Out

"I'm in despair,"
He said.

"How old are you?"
I asked.

"Twenty."

"In that case," I said,
"You've got plenty of time
To find out what despair is really like.
I'm sixty-seven—
I mean, when it comes
To despair.
And that's the easiest way out."

For Peace

The drums
Of the peace-lovers
Don't sound very promising;
Their rhythms are too martial.
In the eyes
Of the peace-lovers
I discover
Hatred.

Time Passes

Yesterday's seventeen-year-old
Will be twenty in three years' time;
The one who is now twenty
In three years he'll be twenty-three.
If the revolution doesn't come soon
They'll all be thirty.

"Please revolution, we beg you
Come soon,
Or we'll have to take a job
And become
Bourgeois."

Remembrance of Great Days

The best things
That May in Paris
Were the graffiti.
They've long been washed off.

That May in Paris
French students
Organized
A nineteenth-century happening.
It was a feast for Romantics.
A feast also for
Revolutionaries grown old
Without ever having had a chance.
They laughed at Jean-Paul Sartre.
Jean-Louis Barrault jumped on the bandwagon
And broke a leg.
What, by the way, became of Cohn-Bendit?
He's making money now.

Demolition of Freedom

How free and superior
The attractive young girl
(Pseudo-pauper of wealthy parents)
Walking the dirty pavement
With naked feet!
And what contempt
Her slender tanned legs radiated!
Until—O cruel fortune—
She stepped on a nail.
Dear child, barefoot
You always step on a nail
When you least expect it.
That's what shoes are for.
Infuriated,
The young beauty limps away.

That reminds me.
In my childhood I went barefoot
From March till late in autumn.
That saved on footwear.
O the marvellous freedom of naked feet!
Except that in October
The toes began to shrink and turn blue.

The dream of my childhood:
A pair of shoes, elegant,
Light brown, with white insoles.
The other day, looking into a display window—
There they were!
I smiled, remembering my faraway dream,
But I didn't buy them.

To Have and Not To Have

There was no dinner
To fill the plates
Of the hungry.

The peace of evening
Did not come to those
Without a roof over their heads.

The night's magnificence
Went unappreciated by the man
Who had no place to sleep.

There are people
Who tremble at the coming of morning—
Not because, as they say,
The world might perish,
But simply because toward morning
It gets bitterly cold.

Kathe Kollwitz: Inexhaustible Faces

No garden. A sky over fields, or flowers? Never.
What she found in the beginning she held fast till the end.
Always the same, always inexhaustible—the human face. And that,
In spite of spring, bright summer, autumn, always only
In a single season: poverty.

The people she knew lived down below,
And they couldn't escape from down below, unless
They were to break from the dark like the Weavers.
But for how long was that? Three days, four?
Those who live down below—they bear.

Just consider: they bear the whole structure of the world,
Patiently, sullenly (always? Things change: be patient!),
And what they bear they know before experience brings it to them,
It's written in their faces; the young know old age, are old already,
But without wisdom—those who live down below know differently.

The man, the son killed in action (but for what cause?),
Accident, sickness, death, pregnancy, and then
A child in her arm. A smile. A child will be a child: it smiles.
That's spring, even if the backyard admits but little light.
At the end—old age; nothing more.

Not a heroic picture. No storms and hardly any movement—
Except for the young man who raised his fist: Never again war!
(That, by the way, was half a century ago.)
Always the same thing; the same, shadow-worn faces
Of those who are more human.

When I met her—this tall, old, withered woman
With her cape and white hair, huddled and chilly
She looked like one of her mothers. And like mine: dignity.
Art moves. It doesn't change anything. In her case:
Yes.

Good Friday

1
It must have been a great poet
Who wrote the story of Peter's denial:
The still night, the ordinary talk
Of the servants, the fire by which
To warm oneself, then unexpectedly
The questions, and in the thin light of dawn
The cock-crow of betrayal,
The glance the two exchanged and no-one else observed.

2
It's all over now:
Arrest, denial, humiliation, the crown of thorns
And the growing exhaustion on the final road—
All accepted and endured.
But when he saw the cross
He trembled—
Quite naturally:
No-one was born for the cross.

3
The palm trees that waved to him
Have long withered away.
He saw through the triumph
Even before he began.
Nothing reaches him anymore.
The cross removes him from everything.
The cross is the sum total, but not the end.

4
The naked body
Duplicates the figure
Of the cross: a leafless tree.
Yet the body is also the tree's
Sole leaf
And sole fruit.
The fruit is taken down and harvested,
The leaf is placed in a cave.
Everything humanly possible is done.
The story is brought to an end.
For today.

How Could I Have Known

How could I have known when I was young?
Young, living deep inside a fire, it was the season of fire—
Knowledge was not party to that green age
When my blazing body was free from aging.

I still hear the voice speak in a whisper:
"Wait till you're old, see what remains of your days of fire."
I still see the face, parched, the disillusioned eyes.
I hardly listened and understood nothing—not then, in the midst of my
  happiness.

What did he mean, that old man with his quavering whisper voice,
Whose years had run away—I don't know, I hardly knew him—?
"Wait," he said, "wait, you'll find out soon enough
How your dreams vanish like windblown clouds."

Time passed and now all things are framed by shadows—
The price of mortality. I don't refuse to pay, I know my debt.
The first sweet light has passed like a breath of air.
Is that first fire out now too?

But then. . . why is it every word now greets me like a ray of morning light?
A smile comes to a face as if I'd never seen one before?
A word, a glance, an outstretched hand—
Why do they burn now with a deeper flame?

The fire that set my early years ablaze is not out yet.
I'm the wood that feeds its flames now—I who came myself from fire
Or from light, the source of which I always seek and know so well.
The shadows are close. I breathe deeply. I burn.

Reflection

When a cigarette has gone up in smoke
You throw away the butt and take a new one.
I wonder if it's possible
To return to earth in some form.
It's not that I'm yearning to come back,
I won't shed any tears
Because I've only been here once.
So much restlessness about trivialities,
So much of being driven. . . and driven. . . .
Would I get anything for nothing in my new life?
Could it perhaps be without partings?
For the time being I go my own way
And I know: this step I'll never take again.
Whatever one does is for the last and for the first time.

When a cigarette has gone up in smoke
You throw away the butt and take a new one.

In the Course of a Week

1

In winter too,
Heaped high with white light
The branches of the tree
Facing my window
Call me outside.

Their confused writing
On the cold blue—
What does it say?

Though hesitantly,
I read in it
Intimations already
Of a heralding
Of faraway spring.

The icy white
Is but a husk,
It merely conceals
The green.

2

In the depth of night
I heard
A hawk's cry—
Here? Is it possible?
O yes: calmly
He drew his circles
In the immeasurable sky
Above the spring meadows
Of my childhood
In the depth of night.

3

I talk
To my shoemaker
As I would talk to
Pasternak, the poet,
Or Saint John-Perse, and
Whoever else it may be.
It's all the same to me.
A glance from the eyes
Of the short Ukrainian
Warms me
No more, no less
Than a line of poetry.
Height and depth don't concern me.
In any case, height
Without depth
Is nothing.

4

Like rain,
Like warm
Earth-opening rain,
The memories
Of my childhood
Fall on me.
Everything in me
Is infinitely refreshed.
I stretch. Strain
Falls from me.
A child grown old.

5
The search for darkness
Is an escape.
It's easy
To play the magician.
Setting off fireworks
Commits you to nothing.
Poets—are you scouts
Or frauds? The despair of our time
Is not despair only.

6
Every morning now
A new beginning:
Will it be the last?
Every night now
A farewell:
Will it be the last?
Between morning and night
The busy
Rounds of the day—
How many more to come?
In the night,
That antechamber of death,
There is sleep—
Isn't there? Who knows? Many
Have departed already.
Never mind: I always expect
Another morning.

7
Resignation is for others.
For me the knowledge
In spite of which
I carry on.

III

A Change of Seasons

I

The stillness this morning
Touched me, in spite of its warmth,
With a cool hand.

In this stillness
Preparations are underway
Without a sound
For the season's changing of the guard.

It's still summer, I say—
But I'm thinking: it'll soon
Be fall.

2

Those that herald autumn
Arrived today—
The crickets in the gardens.

Summer's sun
Never warns you that summer will pass,
But the crickets do,
They tell you:
That's the way it was last year,
And the year before that. . . and before that.
The shadow of a shiver passes over you.

3

The child, long forgotten
But still alive inside me,
Picked up a flaming maple leaf today.

It was this child
Who held the leaf with care
And admired its golden beauty—
While the older man stooped
To gaze with emotion
At its immaculate shape.

It's the same child who'll soon
Be picking up the first chestnut,
Holding its brown coolness
Firmly in his fist—
While the older man drops it
In his pocket with a smile, remembering
An old custom.

4

The red leaf: a spark
Blown here from a still-distant fire.
In my childhood we chased
Across empty fields to find the fire—
It was burning beyond the horizon.

How deliciously bitter its smell was,
How gently exciting its smoke.
The stillness put white threads
Around our necks
And slowly led us back home.

5
How sure of victory,
How aware of her youth,
The beautiful young girl in the morning
Walking across the platform of the subway station—
She must've just returned from summer.
A nymph she was by lakes and rivers,
Or Artemis in the forest, her quiver
Well stacked with arrows.

Artemis, leave me in peace,
Hunt younger and more willing game!

And, let me tell you—
You too will be struck
By autumn.

6
I should look upon all these changes
With jubilant joy,
Because the flame's transformation
Into an intense but calm glow
Is an act of beauty.
But I look upon it
With restrained joy.
Everything is uncertain.
Too many things are unresolved.
And I myself count the years.

All the same: the hour of hours comes
Without a sound.

Past and Present

Many things happened before we came
And the patient earth knows about it.
Many things happened—you read about them
In books, and then you close them.
You can tell them from graves, and then you walk on.
You look at them in museums
And in the end you forget again.
Perhaps it was all too much for the earth,
For this ancient guest-house
Where everyone pays a different price for staying,
And the earth knows all about that too.
But that the two of us are here
And that we give the world something
That never existed before—really
That's something the earth didn't know,
It's something so completely new
That perhaps for that very reason, and solely for us,
The earth has lavished on autumn the splendour of all its fire.

Beginnings

I'm speaking of my father
To whom I owe it
That I write these lines here,
That I own this sheet of paper,
That I can move my hand.
I owe it to him
That I developed an appetite for more than bread
And that I never lost it.
I'm speaking of my father, but
He stands for many.

He explained nothing to me—
Neither the wonder nor the imperfection of the world,
Neither the role he played as carter's man
Nor the roles of other people.
He was too weary for that when he came home,
And he came late every evening, slowly,
Heavily he trudged up the stairs
As if he were carrying sacks filled with the day's ashes.
He hardly ever said anything, he was too tired,
And when he had eaten he fell asleep at the table.
My mother, after a day as a washer woman,
Mended socks and shirts for him and for us all.
With a glance at her old companion she would say:
Don't make so much noise turning the pages.

I sat across from him and read.
I, his son, read for him too.
I was in search of a way, for him too
Whose daily labours made it possible for me
To grasp whole continents
Like fresh, juicy fruit
And drink from them
With insatiable thirst.

Names of Ships

Have you never heard of a ship
That bore the name
ENDURANCE?
It was Shackleton's ship.
It took him to
Ice, silence, suffering and victory
In the Antarctic.
Endurance means triumph.

Have you ever heard of a ship
That bore the name
FRAM?
It was Nansen's ship.
It took him to
Ice, silence, suffering and victory
In the Arctic.
Fram means forward.

Have you heard of a ship
That bore the name
NONPAREIL?
It's your ship,
You'll sail on it
And either go down or triumph.
Nonpareil means unique.

To Take a Trip to Florida

To take a trip to Florida
Doesn't take much time
(Provided you have money and holidays),
Brazil is farther away
But still accessible (given certain conditions).
The North Pole and the South Pole are more difficult
But they're both a possibility (though not for you and me),
And now they talk of the stars.
Those are long journeys—
But are they the longest?
What, for instance, about the journey
Between morning and night
For one who is looking for work?
How long is a day?
Or the journey through his last night
For one who is sentenced to die?
A journey between beginning and. . . what? Future?
Memory and black oblivion.
The length of such journeys cannot be measured.
There's no yardstick for them.

Words

1
Yesterday
I spent my whole
stock of words.
Today
the totally sold-out warehouse
echoes
with my steps
as I search
for a single word.

2
How many
of my words
arrived?
How many, on their way
to other ears, fell
to the ground and withered quickly.
And yet
some must have arrived.
I read it in people's eyes:
eyes acknowledge the receipt of words.
So then it was worth it—
to have spoken.
It is always worth it.
Someone will listen.

3
The second
of two small bronze monkeys
on my desk
(you know: not to see, not
to hear, not to speak)
has his hands over his mouth.
Is he right?

4
But what
would I be
if I didn't speak?
Breath is good.
Breath directed to someone else
is better.

5
And so
I'm sitting
in my totally cleared-out warehouse,
patiently and hopefully
forging new words.
Perhaps they'll last
longer than those
I gave away;
perhaps they'll shine
from deeper inside.
Perhaps they're exactly
the same words as yesterday.
Enough: they'll be words and
they'll be my words—that's
what matters. I shall speak.
I shall utter words
till the last one is gone.
So long as I breathe,
words take shape.
They must be spoken.

6
So be it.
I shall speak again.
I shall do it gladly,
I look forward to tomorrow,
I look forward to saying,
"Good Morning."
That's how it starts.
That's how every day begins.
Speech—that's what it starts with.

7
There are a few words
I can no longer
use so easily,
they've become too precious for me,
I save them
for those who mean much to me,
those I'm fond of—my friends.
Or should one save nothing, should one
offer especially those good words
that are precious?
Even when those words
made from the best materials
are not accepted?
Never mind: someone
will accept them.
Someone will take joy
from what you've made of your breath.

8
On my desk
there always lies
one flawless sparkling
transparent piece of crystal—
one word:
friendship.
In moments of exhaustion
I take it in my hand, and
look—I can feel its warmth.
The rarest crystals
radiate a sublime warmth.

9

Injustice in the world
comes from
not speaking—
don't you remember?
There were times when one
did not speak,
and from that silence grew injustice,
it shot up like weeds
and choked a whole nation.
Nobody spoke up—
that's when a silent nation
(with glorious exceptions)
was cast out of history.

10

There are words
in my mother tongue
which I can no longer use.
I can form them
in another language,
without effort even, but not in my
own, my native tongue, not any more.
I can no longer muster enough breath
for them—the words, if formed,
would choke me.
Curiously, they are words
in my mother tongue.
It's not really curious. I know.

11

Every language
is a continent,
inhabited by friends and lovers,
by killers and frauds,
inhabited by rich and poor, and
by the grey mass between them,
by satiety and hunger,
by light and darkness.
Guess which words,
made from my breath,
and spoken to whom,
keep me alive.

12

How much
wasted breath
lies on our battlefields?
It's the silence
that makes us dumb.

It doesn't have to be
battlefields;
there are other places.
I don't have to name them;
you remember, don't you?
Or must I. . . ?

13

Didn't the world
begin
with a word?
Repeat it.
Say it.
Speak.

14

I shall form
new words
with my breath
like a glass-blower.
Tomorrow I'll give them out—
to you, my friends, to my companions,
and to you whom I don't know.
I shall speak for as long as
I breathe.

Poet of Silence

Words, he said, had lost their meaning.
So he was right to be silent—that is,
He wrote about silence and about
The complete emptiness of words and speech.
After all, poetry of silence was in demand—
O everyone was suffering so fantastically
From the emptiness of words.
Agreed: *chacun à son goût.*

But how did he communicate with his wife
When he wanted breakfast? Or
With his children when they wanted
A story?

What, when the furnace broke down
Or the plumbing—such tiresome
Reminders of petty reality?
How did he talk to the repairman?
Had they agreed on a sign language?

Liar! And, by the way, how long did it take
His ancestors to learn to speak?
Traitor!

Postcard to Certain Young Poets

You seek out the incomprehensible in order to make it comprehensible,
The mystery you understand no better than anyone else
Seems to you more desirable than everyday events.
The mystery repudiates you.

You scrutinize nature through blind spectacles to find false images
  that delight no-one
Because no-one understands them.
Nature repudiates you.

You live in aeons that mean nothing to us because we live today,
You lament the coming end with clouded brow and cry for help and glory,
You are spectators who don't wish to pay admission.
You despise your age, and so the age knows nothing of you.
The age repudiates you.

Still young you already contract stomach ulcers; black bread and water
  you never found delicious;
You avoid speaking of camps, of endless flight, of civil war;
For dictators and barbarism you have but a supercilious smile;
You know nothing of real cold, the room in which you sit is too warm.
Yesterday I saw a drunk come out of a bar, he had his intoxication and
  embraced and cursed the world.
You know neither intoxication nor embrace nor curse.
All you have is paper.
Life repudiates you.

The Much Quoted, Influential Philosopher

The much quoted, influential philosopher,
Whose books on the impending doom of the world
Had been translated into many different languages
And interpreted and annotated by many eager followers,
Angrily closed his window this bright morning.
The children's voices in the garden disturbed him,
The noise of the workmen in the street
Interfered with his thinking
About the inevitable end of the world.
In vexation he turned away
When he saw one workman with a laugh
Toss a cigarette to another.
He walked on different roads
That led to nothingness (in great comfort, of course,
Because those who're hungry don't talk of the end of the world—
They want to be fed),
While the workmen patiently repaired the road,
For him too.

Paroles Essentielles

1

On the slip of paper on my desk
There are no mottoes or maxims;
I've simply made a note of what I need
To buy when I go shopping:
Bread, vegetables, meat,
Onions, tobacco, coffee, milk,
And stamps to send letters to my friends.
Also a bottle of whisky, because I live in Canada,
Also a newspaper, heavier than usual,
And I have to pick up the laundry.

As I write down these words I see
My mother sitting at the kitchen table, in her hand,
Worn down from too much washing, a pencil stump,
Making a list of what we needed for Saturday and Sunday.
She pondered every item. Sometimes
She would cross one out again. Slowly.
It was too expensive and therefore
Not for us.

2

Paroles essentielles:
Mallarmé searched for them.
Here they are:
Bread, milk, meat. Translate them
Into the languages of those who go hungry today.
Essential words—there they are.
And others?: To get enough to eat.
Why did Mallarmé rack his head and heart
When they are so obvious?
I'm a rich man:
I shall buy every item on my shopping-list.
To whom do I owe this?

Big Words

Big words
Turn
My stomach.
It's a diet
I can't digest.
I eat myself well
On little words.

Big Events

Big events are in the making, it's true,
And I believe it because I've read about it
The way you read about such things—
As sleep begins to flow between the lines like black water.

Met an old man
As I was going into town this evening;
He saw me and stopped me
And said—no, he said nothing, before
He could bring out a word I knew
What of all things in the world would do him good.

And the little that I gave him I gave easily.
It wasn't much, wish it could've been more.
And I was ashamed
That in big times such as ours
Old people must suffer from the glory of peace.
Buy yourself a bottle, old man, and recover for an hour.
Big times have always been too big for people like us.

Reading the Story of Sisyphus

Did Sisyphus never tire?
When and how did he rest?
On the side of the hill,
The stone's weight on his shoulders?
When he was permitted to rest
What did he dream? Of the stone
That he would have to move again in the morning?
Why did he never rebel?
Why didn't he let the stone roll
Wherever it would go so that in the depth
He knew so well he could hear it
Land with a crash? Why didn't he
Laugh as if he had lost his senses:
At last, at last, at last I'm rid of my stone?
Why did he never cry out:
I refuse, I refuse, I refuse?
But he was in Hades.
Which Hades?
But there was the decree of the gods.
What gods?
Sisyphus, think!
Sisyphus! Throw off the stone!

Sage People

The eskimo
In this country,
I am told,
Laugh at misfortune.
I'll choose them
For my teachers.
But then I still have
A lot to learn.
I hesitate. Laughter—
That would be too much;
I still have a long way to go.
From far away the voice of
Marcus Aurelius is for me:
Equanimitas.

About Myself

When I was here
To weave the pattern of my life
Into the grand design of uselessness,
When I was here
I received love, and I returned love,
Perhaps more than I received,
Because I was much in need of
Kindness and affection.
I was hunted, occasionally I was hunter too.
I caused tears, and my own tears were my reward.
If anyone took a shot at me, I shot back and sometimes scored,
Because occasionally I heard a doleful sound in the thicket—
But I walked on.
In the distance of my days
I could see Christ and the other people on earth
And I could read clearly in their faces:
What are you doing? Is that what we meant? Follow us!
And I,
Desperate that what they demanded
Was impossible,
Lost myself in the wilderness they call "the world."

Dreamer, They Call Me

Dreamer, they call me;
Calm and untroubled I cast off the label—
What they say no longer concerns me.
Yes and yes and yes again!
I shall keep what you call dreams
Alive until the end of my days,
I who know what you call reality,
I who have the dream.
I shall dream ever more passionately,
Ever more ambitiously, and when I
Close my eyes, I shall be sorry
That I cannot go on dreaming.
Or will that be the beginning
Of yet more magnificent, infinite dreams?

But I don't want to rely on
What no witness has ever reported.
It's entirely enough for me to be here,
Here on earth I want to dream.

Dreamer, they call me;
If only they knew—
I dream with my eyes wide open:
Nothing escapes me.

When the Trumpets Shall Sound

When the trumpets shall sound
On that much invoked Day of Judgment—
What shall I do?
I shall go on sleeping.

When the voice that penetrates all
Breaks into every silence
And guilt is weighed against kindness,
I shall go on sleeping.

When the mighty voice forces me
To admit guilt and plead for mercy
I shall whisper groggy with sleep: I know—
Love and hatred and error and murder and tears and smiles—but now
Let me sleep.

Then for a moment
There'll be silence—
That kind of judge has to think too—
And then the voice of judgment
Will be as kind as a breath of wind in a tree:
You may sleep now forever and ever.

A Day Saved

1
This evening,
Shortly before going to bed,
My head already clouded with sleep,
Lazily, cheerlessly turning the radio dial—
Suddenly
The most marvellous cock-crow:
Mozart!
The day was saved.

2
The night
Became a winter tree
In which a bird sang:
Mozart.
I saw the miracle
With my own eyes,
I swear I saw it:
In the middle of a Canadian winter,
A wind blowing from Labrador,
Everything turned green,
Forest-green, sea-green, meadow-green,
Green as June—
A giant green flag
Unfurled above the frozen world.

3
Where Mozart lies buried,
The earth should really be
Transparent.
The clay should be light
As the air of a summer's day.
It is, it is—
Transparent and light.
Go and see for yourself.
Take the soil in your hand:
It sings.

Strange Sounds

The incessant falling
Of rain on the roof
Outside my window at night—
Like the non-stop hurried
Patter of birds' feet.
Black sparrows, starlings, pigeons—
What precious grains are you picking
In the softly-rushing night?
And why so still
When the harvest is so rich?
But there are only the quick feet,
Only the night rain falling.

The Thrushes Do Not Die Out

I

They have hunted down
The poet.
Yes, they have killed him,
The good-for-nothing, him
Who irritated everybody.
All the nine-to-five men,
All the dutiful housewives—
They have disposed of him.
Yes, like the boy with a slingshot
Who shatters the flight of the thrush
And then, with a shrug,
Kicks
The dead songs into a ditch—
That's how they killed him.
They couldn't bear to hear him sing
While they slaved
To pay off their mortgages
On the house, on the car,
On their lives.
Yes, they have killed him.
There he lies now in a ditch, now
Their world is exactly
The kind of world they want:
A godforsaken place, good
For making money, good
For growing fat and old without joy.
That's what they wanted, they have no
Regrets at all. They killed him
To get rid of him.
He disturbed them: he wasn't like them.

2

Later a scholar found
A bunch of manuscripts
In the ditch—that is to say
In a miserable room,
And he had them published
With his own assiduous annotations:
He had discovered a dead poet
Ignored by his contemporaries.
There you are, they said,
We always knew there was something,
Something quite special in his voice.
Only, why wasn't he like us,
Regular, from nine to five?
He could've made a decent living.
The domestic animals said to the thrush:
Live without wings,
Fly without song.

3

Still later
They put up a statue to him
And the speaker,
A regular nine-to-five man,
Talked of the eternal
Poet.
Everyone felt elevated.

4

The time came
When no-one any longer paid
Any attention to the statue.
Occasionally a thrush
Would settle on his shoulder
And sing into the dead ear
Of the poet.

5
Later still
A young man discovered
The dead poet's verses
And said, why did I
Not know him? He would've been
My friend.
Yes, he is my friend, I will
Follow in his footsteps, I will
Sing, I will
Not be a nine-to-five man.
Ah, my dead friend, he called out,
You have lit up the world for me.

6
Then they started the hunt
All over again.
They will bring him down all right,
Yes, not to worry,
They will kill him.
This, they say,
Is no place for thrushes.

7
But the thrushes
Do not die out.

Barlach's 'Singing Man'

He sat by himself, and yet he was in the world,
Right in the centre of it, where everything comes together,
And where he was equidistant from all other places.
It was then that the breath in his mouth turned into song,
Simply because at that moment he felt like singing.
For him the stars were shining on the earth even on a cloudy day,
And if it was autumn, it was summer too, and spring.
Ah—thus he leaned far back into his singing
And closed his eyes, because he could see better with lowered lids.
He sang, and singing without listeners was happiness to him.

O good old rare and scarcely found word!
He sat on the ground, unstrained, and was there, and elsewhere too.
He was alive because he sang and because he was alive he sang.
In his singing he was all there.

Contents